Nature
Numbers

by Amy Lake

illustrated by John Hovell

HOUGHTON MIFFLIN   BOSTON

Printed in China

ISBN 10: 0-618-88606-0
ISBN 13: 978-0-618-88606-7

15 16 17 18 19 0940 21 20 19 18 17
4500648149

Rain falling gently.

Melting winter's ice.

How many flowers do you see?

Count each flower once, not twice.

Read • Think • Write Now double that number; how many do you get?

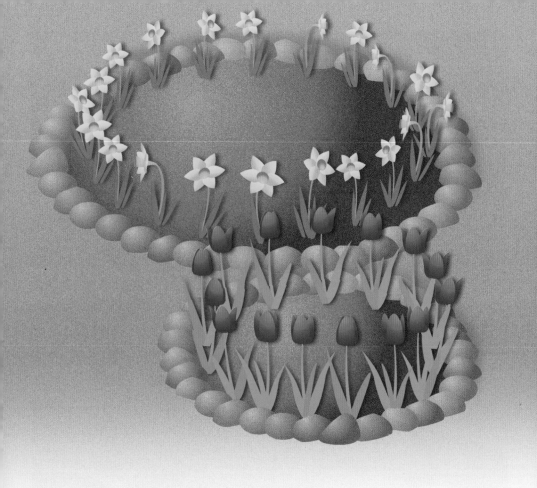

Flowers pushing upward.
The first sure sign of spring.
Count the yellow daffodils.
Then add the tulips to the ring.

Read • Think • Write How many flowers do you see all together?

Birds flying overhead.
Brown pelicans everywhere.
White gulls join them in the sky.
Summer's finally here.

Read • Think • Write   How many birds are in the sky?

Autumn winds are blowing.
Leaves begin to fall.
Time to rake in piles.
Then run, jump, and sprawl.

Read • Think • Write How many piles are there in all?

Winter's 'round the corner.

Squirrels gather on the ground.

Squirrels gather in the trees.

How many squirrels are all around?

Read • Think • Write Now double the number; how many do you get?

Rabbits leave their footprints.
Trails upon the snow.
One rabbit going fast.
And one rabbit going slow.

Read•Think•Write How many footprints did
they make?

Spring Flowers

Show

Look at page 3. Draw the daffodils and tulips you see. Draw yellow X's to show the daffodils and red X's to show the tulips.

Share

Draw Conclusions Talk about the daffodils and tulips on page 3. Tell how to find the total number of flowers.

Write

Write a number sentence to show the total number of flowers on page 3.